A BUSINESS APPROACH TO BEAN FARMING

Complete Entrepreneurial Step By Step Guide To Bean Garden From Scratch

ZHURI HART

DISCLAIMER

This book is intended to provide general information and insights on adopting a business approach to farming. The content within is based on the author's knowledge and experiences up to the date of publication. It is essential to recognize that the field of agriculture is dynamic, influenced by various factors such as market conditions, climate, and regulatory changes.

Readers are advised to conduct thorough research, seek professional advice, and consider their unique circumstances before implementing any strategies or practices discussed in this book. The author and publisher disclaim any responsibility for the accuracy, completeness, or suitability of the information provided. The book is not a substitute for professional advice, and the author and publisher shall not be liable for any damages or losses arising from the use or reliance on the information presented herein.

Individual results may vary, and success in farming enterprises is contingent upon numerous variables. The author encourages readers to consult with relevant experts, agricultural extension services, and legal or financial professionals to tailor strategies to their specific needs and local conditions.

This book is not intended to be a comprehensive guide to all aspects of farming, and readers should exercise their judgment and discretion in applying the principles discussed. The author and publisher do not endorse any specific products, services, or companies mentioned in this book unless explicitly stated.

By reading this book, the reader acknowledges and accepts the inherent uncertainties in agricultural endeavors and agrees to use the information at their own risk.

TABLE OF CONTENTS

ABOUT THE BOOK

A business-oriented and strategic manual for anyone looking to start a bean farm is "A Business Approach to Bean Farming," which is written for both individuals and business owners. This book's significance is in its capacity to provide readers with the fundamental knowledge and abilities required to launch and run a profitable bean farming operation.

The thoughtfully chosen information covers a wide range of topics related to bean farming, from the fundamentals of bean varieties and their traits to the complexities of marketing tactics, sustainable methods, and financial planning.

By exploring the history of bean growing, highlighting the importance of beans in agriculture, and describing the particular goals of the book, the introduction section offers a strong basis. This prepares the ground for a thorough examination of several bean types, their traits, cultivation circumstances, and consumer demand.

After that, the book walks readers through the planning stage of bean farming, going over important topics such as crop rotation techniques, site selection, soil preparation, and climate concerns.

The book's thorough discussion of bean-growing practices, including seed selection, planting procedures, irrigation, fertilization, and pest management, is one of its strongest points. The book gains practicality from its emphasis on crop management, which covers post-harvest handling, trimming, weeding, and harvesting techniques.

To help reader's approach bean farming with a good financial perspective, the financial planning section also offers insightful information on cost analysis, budgeting, funding possibilities, and return on investment strategies.

The book explores marketing tactics, from comprehending the bean industry to successfully branding beans and cultivating relationships with purchasers, going beyond the farm gates.

It also recognizes the significance of offline and online marketing strategies in the cutthroat agriculture environment of today.

Acknowledging the increasing significance of sustainability, a section of the book is devoted to environmental factors in bean production. It addresses sustainable techniques, organic bean farming, and certification choices, bringing the material into line with the growing consumer demand for agricultural products that are produced ethically and environmentally.

Furthermore, the book's practical orientation is demonstrated by the inclusion of a section on obstacles and solutions. Through addressing typical problems in bean farming and offering solutions, the book equips readers to deal with market uncertainty and come out on top in the face of swings.

Finally, for anyone wishing to enter the bean farming industry with a strategic attitude, "A Business Approach to Bean Farming" is an essential resource.

It is an excellent resource for anyone hoping to transform their bean farming activities into profitable and long-lasting enterprises because of its comprehensive examination of numerous facets of the industry combined with useful insights and answers.

CHAPTER ONE

BEAN FARMING INTRODUCTION

THE HISTORY OF BEAN FARMING

The history of bean growing is intricately woven into the pages of agricultural history. Legume crops like beans have been cultivated for thousands of years, demonstrating their ongoing value in many different cultures. Bean farming has its roots in the Middle East, Africa, and Latin America, when native populations realized the usefulness and nutritional worth of these legumes. Beans have been a mainstay in meals all across the world for a long time. They have shaped agricultural techniques and helped feed a variety of cultures.

THE IMPORTANCE OF COFFEE IN AGRICULTURE

Since beans have so many advantages for farmers and ecosystems, they are extremely important to agriculture. Members of the Fabaceae family, including beans, are well known for their capacity to fix nitrogen. Because of this special quality, beans can grow symbiotic partnerships with bacteria that fix nitrogen, which increases the fertility of the soil. This phenomenon helps crop rotation tactics that benefit later plantings as well as the health of the current farming region.

Because beans can add nitrogen to the soil, they are a valuable component of sustainable agricultural operations, which are in line with the increasing emphasis on ecologically friendly farming practices worldwide.

Additionally, beans are essential for human nutrition and food security. These legumes are a vital part of well-balanced diets since they are a great source of fiber, protein, and other important elements.

As an affordable and sustainable source of protein, beans are a beneficial substitute for animal protein in areas where access to it is restricted. As a dependable and reasonably priced source of nourishment, beans are especially important in developing nations when it comes to combating malnutrition and advancing food security.

Apart from their nutritious importance, beans support biodiversity since they come in a variety of kinds that can adapt to varying soil and climate conditions. The variety of bean species—from kidney beans to chickpeas—allows for production in a broad range of settings, improving agricultural resilience. Because beans can be grown in a variety of environments, they are particularly adaptable to climate change and help to maintain the stability of world food production.

The history of human agriculture is entwined with the backdrop of bean growing, demonstrating the crop's universal significance throughout all eras and civilizations.

Beyond their use as a wholesome food source, beans are important to agriculture because of their contributions to soil fertility, sustainable farming methods, and global food security.

Gaining an appreciation of the agricultural and historical aspects of bean farming is necessary to recognize its significance in the present and its potential to fulfill the changing needs of our agricultural systems in the future.

CHAPTER TWO

RECOGNIZING DIFFERENT TYPES OF BEANS

COMMON BEAN TYPES

Legumes that are different in terms of size, shape, and color include beans. Kidney beans, black beans, pinto beans, navy beans, garbanzo beans (chickpeas), and lentils are a few of the most popular varieties of beans. Every cultivar has a distinct texture, flavor character, and culinary use. Kidney beans are frequently included in chili recipes because of their unique form and rich red color.

Black beans are often used in Latin American and Caribbean cuisines due to their creamy texture and dark color. Mexican recipes like refried beans frequently call for pinto beans, which are light brown with speckled patterns. Small and white navy beans are frequently used in stews and soups. Round and beige, garbanzo beans are a mainstay in Middle Eastern and Mediterranean cooking.

Available in a range of hues, including red, brown, and green, lentils are adaptable and utilized in several recipes.

FEATURES AND GROWING ENVIRONMENTS

Bean types differ greatly in size, shape, color, taste, and texture, among other attributes. Furthermore, beans show flexibility and a wide range of growing circumstances. For best growth, most beans need full sun and well-drained soil that ranges from slightly acidic to neutral. However, depending on the type of bean, certain conditions could change.

For example, lentils can withstand colder conditions, but black beans and kidney beans do better in warm areas. Beans are useful to soil fertility because they have a symbiotic interaction with nitrogen-fixing bacteria that allows them to fix nitrogen in the soil. While having enough water is essential for growth, too much moisture can cause illnesses. Crop rotation is frequently advised to ward off pests and illnesses carried by the soil. Overall, successful production depends on an awareness of the distinct qualities and ideal growing environments of each bean species.

DIFFERENT BEAN VARIETIES' MARKET DEMAND

Nutritious trends, cultural customs, and regional culinary tastes all have an impact on the market demand for various bean kinds. Kidney beans, black beans, and pinto beans are widely used and in high demand in Western countries for soups, salads, and burritos. Garbanzo beans, sometimes referred to as chickpeas, are becoming more and more well-liked as plant-based diets and Middle Eastern and Mediterranean cuisines become more and more popular. Owing to their high protein content, lentils are becoming more and more popular among health-conscious consumers.

In addition, as customers look for unusual flavors and sustainable food options, the market for specialty beans has grown. Examples of these beans are organic and heritage kinds. To match consumer requests and profit from the popularity of different bean kinds, growers, distributors, and retailers must have a thorough understanding of these market trends. The market for various bean types is expected to remain dynamic as dietary tastes and culinary landscapes continue to change, offering chances for innovation and expansion in the agricultural sector.

CHAPTER THREE

HOW TO PLAN A BEAN FARM

CHOOSING A SITE AND PREPARING THE SOIL

Carefully choosing your location and properly preparing the soil is essential to the success of your bean farm. Pick a spot that gets lots of sunlight—ideally six to eight hours a day in direct sunlight. Beans want well-drained soil, so stay away from low-lying spots where water can collect. Test the soil to determine its pH, nutritional content, and structural makeup. In general, beans prefer soil that is slightly acidic (pH range of 6.0 to 7.5) over neutral soil.

Clear the soil of any rocks, trash, or weeds before planting. To enhance soil fertility and structure, add organic matter, such as compost or well-rotted manure. Soil that drains well is essential to avoid becoming soggy, which might hinder the growth of beans. If there are drainage problems with your soil, think about installing raised beds.

CONSIDERING THE CLIMATE

Successful bean production requires an understanding of your local climate. Cultivated throughout the warm season, beans like temperatures between 70°F and 80°F (21°C and 27°C).

Because beans are susceptible to cold temperatures, they must be planted after the last frost date in the spring. If you live in an area where the growing season is short, you might want to start your beans indoors and move them outside when the weather is consistently warm.

To avoid heat stress in regions with hot summers, give your bean plants some shade during the warmest part of the day. Because beans need to be consistently watered throughout the growing season, adequate moisture is also essential for their cultivation. Mulching the area around the plants can help keep the soil moist and prevent the growth of weeds.

CROP ROTATION TECHNIQUES

Maintaining the health of the soil and avoiding the accumulation of pests and diseases that could harm bean plants requires the implementation of an efficient crop rotation strategy. To interfere with the life cycles of pests and illnesses unique to beans, rotate your crop rotation to include crops from other plant families. Because legumes like peas and lentils replenish the soil with nitrogen, they are great rotational crops.

Steer clear of planting beans in the same spot every year to lower the chance of developing soil-borne illnesses like Rhizoctonia or Fusarium. A typical rotation cycle involves substituting grains or brassicas for beans. This improves the general health of the soil and breaks the cycle of disease and pests. To guarantee a methodical and long-lasting approach to your bean farming pursuits, maintain a record of your crop rotation strategy.

CHAPTER FOUR

METHODS OF GROWING BEANS

CHOOSING AND PREPARING SEEDS

The selection of seeds is a critical factor in determining the crop's overall success in bean cultivation. High-quality seeds with desirable characteristics including disease resistance, climate adaptability, and high production potential should be chosen first by farmers. For the best germination rates, proper seed preparation is equally crucial. To prevent soil-borne illnesses, this entails applying fungicides or insecticides to seeds. Furthermore, soaking seeds in water before planting can increase the rate of germination and encourage consistent emergence of seedlings.

PLANTING TECHNIQUES

In bean farming, several planting techniques are used based on the kind of bean, the climate where the beans are grown, and the available resources. Transplanting and direct seeding are common techniques. Direct seeding is the process of directly sowing seeds into the ground, either by row planting or disseminating. On the other hand, transplanting entails raising seedlings in a nursery before moving them into the field. The kind of soil, the environment, and the intended yield should all be taken into account when selecting a planting technique.

MANAGEMENT OF WATER AND IRRIGATION

For bean farming to be successful, efficient irrigation and water management are essential since beans need a steady and sufficient supply of water for development and output. Depending on the conditions in the area, farmers may use a variety of irrigation techniques, such as sprinkler, drip, or furrow irrigation. It is crucial to plan irrigation times according to the crop's developmental stages and water requirements, taking into account variables like rainfall patterns and soil moisture content. An increase in bean yield is a result of effective water management, which also guarantees effective water consumption and helps avoid water logging.

EMBRYOLOGY PROCEDURES

One essential element of bean farming that affects plant development, growth, and production is fertilization. Soil testing ought to be done before planting to determine nutrient levels and direct fertilizer delivery. In general, beans gain from a well-balanced fertilizer that includes vital elements like potassium, phosphorus, and nitrogen. To improve soil fertility, organic fertilizers like compost or well-rotted manure can be applied. Fertilizer application must be done at the proper times and in the proper amounts during the bean life cycle to maximize yields and encourage healthy plant development.

CONTROL OF PESTS AND DISEASES

Controlling illnesses and pests is essential to productive bean farming. To reduce the need for chemical pesticides and encourage sustainable practices, integrated pest management (IPM) techniques should be implemented. To spot such problems early on, it's critical to conduct routine pest and disease surveillance. The accumulation of pests and illnesses can be avoided by rotating crops, using resistant cultivars, and keeping plants spaced properly. Farmers can, if needed, use selected pesticides or biological control techniques to address certain problems with the least amount of negative environmental effects. Furthermore, maintaining high hygiene in bean fields might help lower the likelihood of pest and disease outbreaks by eliminating crop waste, for example.

CHAPTER FIVE

MANAGEMENT OF BEAN CROPS

PRUNING AND TRAINING

Two crucial elements of managing bean crops successfully are pruning and training. To improve the general health of the plant, pruning entails removing undesired or excess plant material, such as dead or diseased branches. Pruning is very crucial for bean crops to preserve the ideal canopy structure, which improves airflow and solar penetration.

This lowers the chance of illness and encourages better photosynthesis. In contrast, training entails directing the growth of bean plants to produce the appropriate structure. Staking and trellising are common training techniques that support plants and stop them from sprawling. Easier harvesting, better pest and disease management, and higher yields are all influenced by proper pruning and training.

STRATEGIES FOR WEEDING

To guarantee that the plants receive enough nutrients and resources, weeding is an essential part of managing bean crops. Timely removal of undesirable plants or weeds that compete with beans for sunlight, water, and nutrients is an important part of effective weeding tactics. A common technique for controlling temperature, retaining soil moisture, and inhibiting weed growth is mulching. Additionally, hand weeding is frequently done, particularly in the early phases of bean growth when plants are more vulnerable to rivalry. Furthermore, using companion plants as natural weed suppressors during intercropping can be a sustainable practice. To keep weeds out of the way and maximize the health of bean crops overall, it's imperative to combine these weeding strategies.

BEST PRACTICES FOR HARVESTING

Harvesting is a crucial stage in bean crop management that affects yield quantity and quality. Selecting the ideal time to harvest is crucial since too developed and tough beans might result from harvesting too soon, while beans that are harvested too soon may lack flavor and nutritional content. The best time to harvest beans depends on the type of bean and whether they will be dried or consumed fresh. Dry weather is ideal for harvesting to avoid post-harvest illnesses. Sharp harvesting implements provide a clean cut and reduce plant damage. To avoid bruising or damage that could lower the crop's overall quality and market value, the harvested beans must be handled carefully.

POST-HARVEST HANDLING AND STORAGE

These processes are essential to maintaining the grade and market value of produced beans. It is essential to properly dry beans as soon as they are harvested to stop mold formation and preserve the right amount of moisture. Beans should be stored in hygienic, well-ventilated containers to help against fungus growth and insect infestations. Conditions for dry, cool storage are crucial to reduce the chance of bean deterioration.

It's important to regularly check stored beans for any indications of pests or illnesses and to respond quickly if something is wrong. Furthermore, employing breathable bags and other suitable packing techniques guarantees that the beans stay fresh and marketable for a longer amount of time. Farmers eventually profit financially from the longevity and quality of their bean crop, which is greatly enhanced by appropriate post-harvest management and storage techniques.

CHAPTER SIX

BUDGETING FOR THE PRODUCTION OF BEANS

COST ANALYSIS AND BUDGETING

Carefully analyzing expenses and creating a detailed budget are key components of financial planning for bean farming. When evaluating a venture's viability and profitability, cost analysis is essential. This means determining and projecting every possible cost related to growing beans, such as personnel, equipment, irrigation, fertilizers, pesticides, seed procurement, and land preparation. Farmers can better allocate resources by knowing the financial requirements and making well-informed decisions with the help of a comprehensive cost breakdown.

A crucial part of financial planning is budgeting, which helps farmers allocate resources effectively. It helps prevent overspending and resource shortages by offering a road plan for handling costs. Both fixed and variable costs should be included in the budget, taking potential risks and seasonal variations into account. Farmers can improve overall financial performance by setting realistic financial goals, setting aside money for unforeseen expenses, and making well-informed judgments when they implement an efficient budgeting system.

OPTIONS FOR FUNDING AND FINANCING

For a bean farming enterprise to be successful, it is imperative to get sufficient capital. Farmers have access to a variety of finance and financing choices; selecting the best one necessitates carefully evaluating the unique requirements and financial capacity of the farm. Conventional finance alternatives are frequently chosen, including bank loans and agricultural credit agencies. Farmers should, however, look into alternate funding options like private investors, government grants, and agricultural subsidies.

Other options for raising money include agricultural cooperatives and crowd-funding websites. Within the farming community, cooperative efforts might result in pooled resources and lower financial costs. To make an informed decision that supports the long-term financial objectives of the bean farming endeavor, it is imperative to evaluate the repayment terms, interest rates, and eligibility requirements of various funding sources.

STRATEGIES FOR RETURN ON INVESTMENT (ROI)

To guarantee the economic viability of bean farming, cultivators need to devise efficient Return on Investment (ROI) tactics. Evaluating the ROI entails determining how profitable the investment is in comparison to the outlay of funds. To assess the effectiveness of their agricultural operations, farmers need to take into account variables including crop production, market pricing, and input costs.

A positive return on investment can be achieved by implementing sustainable agriculture methods, investing in contemporary technology, and implementing effective resource management techniques. Increasing crop diversity, pursuing specialized markets, and setting up direct-to-consumer sales channels are some tactics that can improve yields. To maximize profitability and accomplish long-term financial success in bean farming, farmers can adjust their methods and make well-informed decisions by tracking and evaluating key performance indicators over time.

CHAPTER SEVEN

ADVERTISING TECHNIQUES

COMPREHENDING THE BEAN MARKET

For enterprises to successfully maneuver through the competitive terrain of the bean market, they must initially grasp the forces that mold this sector. Understanding consumer preferences, new trends, and possible business prospects all depend heavily on market research. Important insights can be gained from examining variables such as the impact of cultural preferences, demographic trends, and regional differences in bean consumption.

Additionally, firms may make more informed judgments if they remain aware of changes in the market, difficulties in the supply chain, and environmental factors. Developing a focused and effective marketing strategy requires a deep grasp of the bean market.

HOW TO BRAND YOUR BEANS

Beans are no different from any other commodity when it comes to the importance of brand identity in a competitive market. It takes more than just a clever logo to create an engaging brand for beans; it also takes a well-considered story those appeals to consumers. Companies should tell the tale of the beans while highlighting attributes like sustainability, quality, and distinctive selling propositions. Using powerful branding techniques, such as maintaining visual consistency on online and packaging materials, can aid in creating a dependable and identifiable brand image. Using storytelling to establish a human connection with customers increases brand loyalty and creates the conditions for long-term market success.

DEVELOPING STRONG RELATIONSHIPS WITH BUYERS

In a market where customer loyalty and preferences are key drivers, developing strong relationships with buyers is imperative. Having open lines of communication and a dedication to fulfilling the demands of distributors, retailers, and end users are key components in developing trust with them. Building trust may be achieved through offering outstanding customer service, open communication about the product, and adaptable teamwork. Businesses can maintain a connection with their audience by using regular communication channels including newsletters, social media engagements, and consumer feedback tools. Comprehending the buyer's journey from the point of product discovery to post-purchase interaction enables customized strategies that improve the customer experience as a whole.

STRATEGIES FOR ONLINE AND OFFLINE MARKETING

To achieve maximum reach and engagement in today's company environment, a comprehensive marketing strategy needs to incorporate both offline and online platforms. A strong online presence that includes a website that is easy to use, active social media accounts, and well-planned content marketing are all part of online marketing strategies. In a competitive digital world, visibility can be improved by utilizing online advertising and search engine optimization (SEO). In addition, offline strategies including taking part in neighborhood gatherings, partnering with physical stores, and using conventional advertising techniques can assist in reaching a variety of consumer demographics. A comprehensive and efficient marketing strategy for beans in the market is ensured by a well-integrated approach that smoothly combines offline and online marketing initiatives.

Achieving success in the bean market requires a diversified strategy that starts with a thorough comprehension of market dynamics. A successful marketing strategy is based on creating a compelling brand story, cultivating strong customer relationships, and utilizing a well-balanced combination of offline and online marketing techniques.

CHAPTER EIGHT

ENVIRONMENTAL ASPECTS AND SUSTAINABILITY

GROWING ORGANIC BEANS

Organic bean farming is a type of farming that places a strong emphasis on growing beans using natural, eco-friendly methods. In contrast to traditional farming, organic bean farming uses organic substitutes that support soil health and biodiversity in place of synthetic fertilizers, herbicides, and insecticides. This approach aims to preserve ecosystem equilibrium by eschewing dangerous chemicals that may have negative impacts on the environment and public health.

ECOLOGICAL METHODS

Organic bean cultivation is essential for reducing the environmental impact of agriculture from the perspective of sustainability. Organic farming lowers the risk of contaminating land and water by eschewing the use of synthetic inputs. Long-term sustainability is further enhanced by the practice's promotion of soil fertility through crop rotation and the application of organic matter. Agroecological concepts, which emphasize an integrated and holistic strategy that promotes harmony between agriculture and the natural environment, are aligned with organic bean cultivation.

Beyond organic farming, sustainable practices in bean farming incorporate a wider range of ideas designed to reduce the environmental impact of agricultural operations. These techniques include reducing waste, using energy efficiently, and conserving water.

Using precision farming methods, such as timed irrigation and well-planned planting, helps reduce resource use and increase productivity. Bean farming systems that incorporate cover crops and agroforestry improve sustainability even further by fostering biodiversity, halting soil erosion, and sequestering carbon.

OPTIONS FOR CERTIFICATION

Options for certification are essential for guaranteeing that organic and sustainable farming methods are used in the production of beans. Farmers must follow criteria and procedures set by various certification agencies, such as the European Union Organic Farming Certification or the United States Department of Agriculture (USDA) Organic Certification. Obtaining certification guarantees that organic agricultural techniques are followed and provide consumers with the assurance that the beans they buy satisfy certain ethical and environmental standards. The certification process helps to increase customer confidence in ecologically friendly and sustainable farming methods, which in turn increases demand for goods that share these ideals.

It should be noted that organic bean growing, sustainable techniques and certification alternatives are all related ideas that are essential to tackling environmental issues in agriculture. Adopting sustainable practices and embracing organic farming techniques improves soil fertility and lessens the ecological impact of farming, all of which benefit ecosystem health. Options for certification serve as a means of verifying compliance with these guidelines, giving customers the peace of mind that the beans they select are grown sustainably and with minimal impact on the environment. When combined, these ideas provide a thorough framework for encouraging bean growing that is more environmentally conscious and sustainable.

CHAPTER NINE

PROBLEMS AND SOLUTIONS

TYPICAL OBSTACLES IN BEAN FARMING

Numerous obstacles that affect bean farming's overall production and viability as a business exist. Infestation by pests is one frequent problem. Aphids, mites, and beetles are just a few of the pests that can seriously harm bean harvests.

To control infestations, farmers frequently need to employ integrated pest management techniques. These techniques include crop rotation, the use of natural predators, and the prudent application of pesticides to minimize environmental damage.

Managing soil fertility is a challenge in bean production. Like many other crops, beans need certain nutrients to flourish to their full potential. Continued farming without enough restocking of the soil can cause nutrient depletion, which will reduce harvests. Sustainably managed soil requires farmers to use techniques like cover crops and adding organic matter to improve soil fertility and preserve long-term yield.

Bean producers have a great deal of difficulty due to unpredictable weather patterns. Extreme weather, drought, and heavy rains can all affect beans. These problems are made worse by climate change, which results in erratic growing seasons and a higher chance of crop failure.

Farmers can invest in irrigation systems, look into climate-resilient bean varieties, and monitor weather patterns to make appropriate decisions to lessen these consequences.

TECHNIQUES FOR SOLVING PROBLEMS

Proactive problem-solving techniques are crucial to tackling the difficulties associated with bean cultivation. Using ecologically friendly methods for pest monitoring, prevention, and control, integrated pest management (IPM) is a comprehensive approach. Farmers can successfully manage pest problems while maintaining the health of the ecosystem by implementing biological controls and reducing dependency on chemical pesticides.

An enhanced method of managing soil fertility is to apply agroecological techniques. Crop rotation, cover crops, and organic farming methods improve soil structure, replenish vital nutrients, and advance general soil health. Furthermore, soil testing can help farmers determine which nutrients are needed in what amounts, allowing for targeted fertilization to maximize bean development.

Choosing bean varieties that are tolerant of changing environmental circumstances is an important part of adapting to climate change. Farmers can work with extension organizations and agricultural researchers to find climate-smart cultivars that are appropriate for their area. Investing in drip or sprinkler systems ensures consistent bean production by offering a dependable water supply during dry spells or irregular rains.

GETTING PAST MARKET VOLATILITY

Bean growers face difficulties due to market changes, which can affect pricing, demand, and overall profitability. Diversification is one tactic to reduce market uncertainty. Farmers can lower their reliance on a single market and diversify the risk by growing a variety of beans or looking into other crops.

It is imperative to establish robust connections with both local and regional markets. Establishing connections with distributors, merchants, and food processors can offer beans a more reliable market outlet. Through processing and packaging, farmers can also investigate value addition, developing specialized products that meet particular customer tastes and possibly fetch greater prices.

Making educated selections requires keeping up with market developments and demand. Farmers who conduct ongoing market research are better equipped to predict changes in customer tastes, modify output levels appropriately, and match their tactics to the needs of the market. In addition, membership in agricultural associations or farmers' cooperatives can give farmers collective bargaining strength, enabling them to better negotiate pricing and manage market uncertainty.

www.ingramcontent.com/pod-product-compliance
Lightning Source LLC
Chambersburg PA
CBHW070837290526
45795CB00002B/896